PLANTS AT YOUR FINGERTIPS

PLANTS FOR THE

DRY
GARDEN

PETER THURMAN

First published in Great Britain in 1994 by
PAVILION BOOKS LIMITED
26 Upper Ground, London SE1 9PD

Conceived, edited and designed by Russell Ash & Bernard Higton
Picture research by Julia Pashley
Plant consultant Tony Lord

A CIP catalogue record for this book is available from the
British Library.

ISBN 1 85793 112 2

Printed and bound in Singapore by Tien Wah Press

2 4 6 8 10 9 7 5 3 1

This book may be ordered by post direct from the publisher.
Please contact the Marketing Department.
But try your bookshop first.

CONTENTS

INTRODUCTION

Water is *the* basic essential for plant life and growth. Not only is it intrinsically involved in all the important chemical reactions that take place in a plant but it also acts as a plant's communication system – a solvent and transport medium for nutrients and other vital substances. Additionally, water produces an internal pressure in a plant, thereby creating its rigid, yet flexible form. As much as 95% of the weight of a plant is made up by water.

Plants lose water through their leaves by evaporation (transpiration) and in so doing also keep cool. The water in the leaves is constantly replaced through a continuous chain of water-containing cells that form a direct link with the roots which, in turn, are in intimate contact with the water in the soil. So long as the water column remains unbroken, water is sucked out of the soil by the sun, via the plant. A large tree in full leaf may draw over 1,600 litres (350 gallons) of water from the soil per day. From all this, it follows that a dry garden – a garden lacking water – can present something of a problem!

CAUSES OF DRYNESS

A dry environment can cause a plant to desiccate because it loses more water through its leaves than it is able to replace from its roots. A dry garden can be caused by any one or a combination of the factors that result in a water shortage in the soil and/or in the air. These can be summarized as:

EUPHORBIA CHARACIAS, LAVENDER AND A YELLOW FELTED FLOWER SPIKE
OF *VERBASCUM* AT DENMANS, SUSSEX.

1. Climate	Low rainfall High temperatures Drying winds Freezing
2. Soil type	Light, sandy soils Shallow soils, especially those over a porous bed rock Heavy, clay soils Low water-table level
3. Site conditions	Exposed, sloping or open aspects. The presence of a rain barrier (such as a high wall) or major competitor for water (such as a large tree or weeds).

1. Climate

In recent years there has been much discussion about global warming and changes in weather patterns. We know that holes in the planet's ozone layer will raise temperatures, causing prolonged droughts in areas that were previously lush. In addition, it is feared that the polar ice-caps will melt, raising the sea level which will flood lowland areas.

Recent abnormal weather conditions in Britain have given these horrific predictions a good deal of credibility. Mild winters and long, hot, dry summers have affected many parts of the country. This is a problem that has had to be tackled by a great many gardeners over these last few years.

Hot weather and low rainfall often go together. These two climatic factors combine to reduce the amount of water in the soil. Low rainfall reduces the quantity of water coming *in* to the soil; high temperatures increase the amount of water *leaving* the soil through evaporation. On a warm summer's day, a bare square-metre of earth will lose around two litres (half a gallon) of water through evaporation. This directly affects the amount of water available to plants.

Wind can also cause soils to dry out not only by direct action but also because it increases water loss from plants via their leaves. Wind reduces the humidity in the air and around the leaves, thereby increasing the 'pull' of water out of the plant and in turn out of the soil. A plant can be damaged by the effect of warm, drying winds even when there is plenty of water in the soil if it cannot extract and transport water sufficiently fast to its stems and leaves to compensate for the increased loss through the foliage. A similar state of affairs can exist when the ground is frozen as the water in the soil is in a form that cannot be taken up. In coastal regions, wind coming off the sea can be laden with salt, which causes more water to leave the plant through exosmosis.

HELIANTHEMUM, LIBERTIA AND EUPHORBIA IN A DRY BORDER.

2. Soil type

The level of moisture in the ground is directly related to soil type and the amount of humus it contains. Humus or organic matter can be simply described as decaying vegetable and animal remains.

Soils are made up of different minerals broken down into minute particles. The three main particle types are sand, silt and clay. They vary greatly in size; sand particles are the largest and clay the smallest. A balanced mixture of these particles creates a garden loam with air pockets containing oxygen and the ability to retain water – both vital for plant growth.

This alone, however, is not enough. Humus must also be present. It has the almost magical and certainly essential ability to bind the various soil particles together to form what is known as a good crumb structure. This not only improves the water-holding capacity and aeration of the soil, but also enables nutrients to be 'held' in a form that plants can use.

Dry soils are often missing this delicate balance of ingredients. For example, they may have a predominance of only one of the particle sizes because the soil is particularly sandy or clayey. Sandy soils have large air pockets that prevent water retention and encourage very free drainage. As a result, nutrients are also leached out quickly.

Clay soils can also be a problem. The minute particles attract and retain a great deal of water. They can be very boggy in winter but as soon as water levels drop the clay particles shrink and bind together to form very hard impermeable plates separated by large cracks. The clay holds on to any moisture very tightly, preventing plant roots from absorbing it. Any water subsequently reaching the soil rushes down the cracks or runs off the surface. Air entering the cracks dries the soil out even faster and so the cracks can deepen. Cracking also tears roots apart causing instability and a reduced root system.

A STEPPED PATHWAY THROUGH WARM SUNNY BEDS WITH *Epilobium*
IN FULL FLOWER IN THE FOREGROUND.

Chalky or alkaline soils break down and use up organic matter very quickly. This is because the bacteria that do most of the work prefer alkaline conditions. As a result, such soils are constantly in danger of losing their capacity to hold water and nutrients.

If the base or bed rock underneath the soil is porous (for example, chalk or sandstone) it will 'soak up' the water that is gravity fed down from the soil, and the soil will have difficulty retaining moisture.

For various reasons certain soils may be quite shallow. The bed rock may be near the surface, either naturally or as a result of erosion. Some soil types break down organic matter quickly which means that the soil has no time to assimilate the organic matter and improve its texture and water-retaining ability. So, if the bed rock is porous *and* near the surface, or if the soil is just shallow and perhaps poor in structure, it is in great danger of drying out.

In some areas of the country the soil water table (the level below which all the pore spaces are water-filled) may just be characteristically low. This is generally true on high or sloping ground or in soils that have been artificially built up. Water landing on a soil surface enters and progressively fills the air pockets between the soil particles. It moves downwards as long as the water supply continues. When the supply stops, the downward movement continues for a time and displaced air is pulled back in. Each soil particle is then surrounded by a coating of water and dissolved nutrients which is readily available to plants – conditions in which plants grow very well. Unfortunately this state of affairs is sometimes not reached as a result of various human factors: watering with a high pressure hose, for example, may smear the soil surface which then forms an impenetrable cap; overuse or trampling can consolidate the soil with the same effect; over-enthusiastic cultivation can produce a dusty surface which becomes a creamy sludge at the first fall of water – miniature pools and rivers may then form which can lead to further capping or, in severe cases, erosion.

3. Site conditions

There can be other, very localized reasons for dryness in a garden. If the garden is sloping, some rain will run off down the gradient before it can be absorbed by the soil. This occurs in particular during heavy rain storms, with the result that, even in an area of high rainfall, a sloping garden may be prone to drying out.

An exposed garden, such as one on the side of a hill, will obviously be more exposed and hence vulnerable to drying winds.

A high wall, fence or overhanging roof above a garden border can act like an umbrella. Rain will be deflected away from the soil and thereby create quite small but nevertheless significant dry patches. Bricks and other walling materials actually absorb some soil water themselves, though a damp-proof course will minimize this.

Similarly, dry conditions may occur under a large tree, especially if it is a thirsty species such as willow or poplar. Not only will the tree act as a rain shield, particularly when

LAMIUM PROVIDING GROUND COVER IN DRY SHADE.

in leaf, but will also use most of the available soil water itself. Trees with a shallow root system and an abundance of surface roots will be especially guilty of this. Weeds sprouting around newly planted trees or shrubs compete for water, nutrients and rooting space to such an extent that the plant may die.

SYMPTOMS OF DRYNESS

Along with water, the basic requirements for healthy plant growth are light, air and nutrients. If any one of these factors is out of balance with the rest, growth is adversely affected. The principle of limiting factors means that plant health and growth is controlled and restricted by the most limiting essential requirement.

It is no good if light and nutrients are in plentiful supply if water is lacking. Plants cannot make use of an abundance of any one growth factor if another is scarce. The result is stress. A plant suffering from a lack of water (water stress) from whatever cause will show certain symptoms.

In order for plants to take up nutrients, they must be in solution. In dry conditions, therefore, nutrients are less available, so plants may look hungry. The leaves may be smaller and paler in colour. Growth will be slow or may even stop completely. The leaves will appear dull and will quickly show that all is not well by wilting.

The drop in water pressure in the plant has the same effect as the drop in air level in a balloon. The leaves and young stems will shrink in size and start to droop. Initially, flowering and fruiting can actually be improved. Lack of water causes various changes in a plant's metabolism which in turn prompt it to produce flowers and then seed in an attempt to perpetuate the species. All the protein and energy is diverted away from useless leaf and stem growth and into the production of offspring. Many commercial growers use water stress to induce plants to flower or fruit earlier, and you may notice vegetables running to seed prematurely. Long periods of moderately dry conditions however, will exhaust the plant and reduce flowering, fruiting and life expectancy.

If the water shortage continues to worsen, all parts of the plant, including the roots, become hardened and green parts, especially the leaves, start to turn brown and drop off. This can expose the plant to further damage by diseases. At this stage plants can look pretty sorry for themselves – to the inexperienced gardener they may appear beyond help.

Although some die-back of stems and roots may have occurred, the application of water at this stage will resuscitate a plant. Eventually, however, if a serious lack of water persists, a point of no return is reached and no amount of water will revive the plant.

Drying winds cause a slight variation in symptoms. The browning or scorching of leaves becomes the prevalent indicator, in the early stages only on the windward side. A dry atmosphere, especially in greenhouses, may also cause buds and flowers to drop off prematurely or prevent fruit development. Fortunately, there is a great deal that a gardener can do to alleviate the problems associated with dry conditions and a dry garden.

THE SOLUTIONS

There are many ways of improving a dry garden. They can be summarized as follows:
1. Soil improvement
2. Mulching
3. Weed control
4. Creating shelter
5. Garden design alterations
6. Changing or improving cultivation techniques
7. Water conservation and irrigation systems
8. Plant selection

A SHRUB BORDER MULCHED WITH COCONUT WASTE.

1. Soil improvement

Getting your soil into good shape is probably the single most important weapon available with which to fight dryness.

If your soil is a good friable loam with abundant organic matter you will not suffer too badly, even in a severe drought. However, if your soil is clay or sandy or like any of the other 'problem' types described previously, then a long, hot summer may result in plant deaths.

Improving your soil is simple: you just need to add organic matter to it. Organic matter is defined as any decayed vegetable or animal matter. Organic matter has the ability to retain moisture in its own right and improves the soil structure. Clay soils are broken up by it, which improves aeration and drainage during the winter months. In summer, cracking is prevented and water available to plant roots is held by the organic matter itself. Well-drained, sandy or gravelly soils, on the other hand, are bound together by the incorporation of organic matter. This makes them better able to hold water for use by plants. Shallow soil will increase in bulk by the application of organic matter.

There are various sources of organic matter, the most obvious being your home-made compost from garden waste and leaf mould. You will find other types available depending on the locality. In most rural areas, horse manure from stables or pig and cow manure from farms will be for sale. Mushroom farms will supply mushroom compost and hop growers spent hops. Chicken-house litter, sewerage sludge and, near the coast, seaweed, can also be obtained.

Fresh manure should not be used because it may contain toxic levels of some elements. Make sure it is old, or allow it to stand for a few months, ideally mixed with straw or sawdust which helps to 'dilute' it. As well as improving the soil's water-retaining properties, manures also supply some important plant nutrients.

On heavy clay soils the application of coarse grit, which breaks up the clay very effectively, should be considered.

The use of sphagnum moss or peat is no longer considered to be environmentally friendly. It is a finite resource and its exploitation directly threatens plants and animals that are unique to the peat bog habitat. Consequently, the commercial peat packagers have been forced to develop alternatives. Bi-products of the forestry industry, such as composted bark and coconut fibre from the Far East, known as coir, are suitable substitutes for improving your soil.

Organic matter can be applied directly to the surface (as a mulch) or better still dug into the soil. Either way the soil is able to hold more moisture for plants during dry or windy periods. Remember also that plant nutrients need to be in solution for plants to take them up and benefit from them, so adding organic matter that improves a soil's moisture holding capacity also increases the food supply.

2. Mulching
A mulch is any material applied to the soil surface to reduce water loss through evaporation and to moderate the soil temperature.

Annual weeds are suppressed and, with organic mulches, nutrients are supplied and the soil structure improved as the mulch breaks down. Smearing and compaction of the soil surface may also be reduced.

Organic mulches include most of the types of organic matter mentioned under soil improvement. In addition, wood or bark chips make an excellent mulch that lasts for a number of years before breaking down. Composted bark, wood and bark chips use up nitrogen from the soil as they break down. Provided it has been bought from reputable suppliers, however, this should not be a problem as a source of nitrogen should have been added to compensate for this loss.

Inorganic mulches include stones, gravel, polythene sheeting or even pieces of old carpet. Those that could look unsightly can be restricted to the vegetable garden or hidden by a layer of organic mulch.

In recent years, various proprietary brands of geo-textile sheeting or planting membranes have been marketed. These materials, usually purchased on a roll or in sheets, are porous to rainwater but stop weed growth. When they are covered with bark you have the ultimate mulch.

By moderating the soil temperature, mulches provide the added bonus of insulating the soil in winter. This prevents plant death from cold and from 'drought' conditions caused by the freezing of the soil water.

3. Weed control

Weeds compete for all the plant growth requirements – light, air, nutrients and of course water. Keeping weeds down will obviously increase the amount of water available for your plants. Regular hoeing is the usual method of weed control during the growing season – especially with annual weeds.

Perennial weeds like bindweed and ground elder can be difficult to eradicate. The best method is to dig out as much of the root as possible in the winter months and then spot treat with a

A *BERBERIS* HEDGE ACTING AS A WIND BREAK.

carefully applied systemic weed killer through the spring and summer. A systemic weed killer is one which is taken down into the plant and kills the roots. A contact weed killer kills only the green parts, which is enough to get rid of young or annual weeds, but is not wholly effective on perennials.

If you don't like using chemicals then physical removal by fork or by hand is the only alternative.

A mulch will suppress weeds but will not make them magically disappear – especially perennial types. It is best to get rid of as many weeds as possible and then apply a mulch.

4. Creating shelter

If you live in an exposed, windy area, perhaps at high altitude or in a coastal region, creating some form of shelter will not only reduce water loss from the soil and plants but also make your garden more relaxing and peaceful.

Solid barriers are inadvisable because they only deflect the wind, causing turbulence rather than protection. The ideal windbreak has to be semi-permeable, acting as a filter by allowing the wind to pass through but reducing its velocity.

There are two basic types of windbreak: living and artificial. Living windbreaks are hedges, or, on a larger scale, shelter-belts. Hedges and shelter-belts are relatively cheap, attractive and long-lived but in a dry garden they will add to the problem by extracting water themselves.

Artificial windbreaks, usually made of some sort of mesh or netting, are more expensive and less attractive but they are movable – and they do not need water! They are particularly good for protecting new plantings and help to speed up establishment.

Just one section of trellis, perhaps covered with a square of netting, will shelter a small corner or a particularly cherished specimen. In coastal regions, windbreaks or hedges will collect up the salt as well as reducing wind speed.

5. Garden design alterations
Water conservation and shelter can be improved by making some changes in the layout of your garden.

Breaking up the garden into a series of 'outdoor rooms' will increase shelter and conserve water. This can be achieved by trellis or carefully chosen fencing or hedging.

Terracing a sloping site into smaller, level areas will reduce surface water run-off. It can be an expensive operation but the results, both visually and as far as moisture conservation is concerned, will be very worthwhile.

On a hot summer's day a bit of shade is most welcome – not only to us but also to the plants. In a suitable position a carefully chosen tree that is not too thirsty can actually reduce water loss from nearby plants.

During a long, hot summer, lawns can be a parched, brown dust bowl. In certain situations it may be worthwhile considering an alternative material. The lawn could be reduced in

A *PHORMIUM* WITH YUCCAS AND *POTENTILLAS* IN GRAVEL.

size – part of it near the house may be turned into an exten-
sion of the patio. If the grass under the tree has always been
poor – turn it into a border of shade and dry-tolerant plants
(see Checklists). Other portions of the lawn could be
converted to a gravel area. Constructed properly, with a
weed-suppressing membrane underneath, these areas can be
maintenance-free and add a new dimension to your garden

Gravel gardens can be colonized by drought-tolerant plants
that seed themselves around and provide an informal, weed-
free area that will not suffer from the rigours of dry periods.

Lastly, a psychologically beneficial garden feature for a dry
garden is water. The sound of a gentle trickle of water from a

LAVENDER, *STACHYS* AND YUCCA IN THE GERTRUDE JEKYLL AND EDWIN LUTYENS GARDEN AT HESTERCOMBE, SOMERSET.

small waterfall or spout creates a cooling atmosphere. A self-contained feature re-cycles the same water continuously and needs only to be topped up occasionally to compensate for evaporation.

6. Changing or improving cultivation techniques

Planting in autumn rather than spring can have many benefits. The ground is still warm and root growth is possible through to winter. This early establishment reduces losses if the the following summer is dry. In spring the ground takes time to warm up and if early root growth is negligible and is followed by a severe natural drought, failures will result. Plants that have adapted to dry conditions in their natural environment may, however, prefer not to have to endure winter so soon after planting. The combination of cold and wet before full establishment can prove fatal, so plant these types in spring. When planting in spring or summer – summer bedding plants, for example – soak the plants and the hole first. Once planted, prune the plant back to reduce early water loss.

When you plant a shrub or tree in a lawn, create a round bed of its own to eliminate competition from the grasses for water and nutrients.

During a drought, mow a lawn only when necessary and raise the cutting height on your lawnmower. Allow the clippings to stay on the surface to conserve moisture. This will build up a 'thatch' around the grass roots, but it can be scarified out in the autumn. Stop feeding your lawn, to reduce growth and remove competitive weeds.

To reduce watering of plants in pots or hanging baskets, add a water-absorbing gel to the compost. This acts like a sponge – soaking up and holding a great deal more water for plant use.

7. Water conservation and irrigation systems

Hose-pipe bans in some parts of the country have become an annual inevitability and the water authorities are progressively installing water meters in order to reduce household consumption. So here are some tips on how best to conserve water and avoid wastage when watering:

Always water in the evenings when it is cooler. This reduces evaporation, and the danger of leaf scorch caused by the water droplets behaving like a magnifying glass on the foliage.

Water thoroughly and less frequently rather than little and often. This ensures that the moisture level in the soil is increased to a decent depth rather than just the surface layer. The development of surface roots, which are prone to drying out, is therefore discouraged.

Do not use a high pressure jet on a hose or the various oscillating or arching sprinklers. They are inaccurate and wasteful. Have the water just trickling out of the hose and direct it at the base of the plant.

If you make a ridge of soil around the stem of a plant, you create a min-reservoir which gives the soil time to absorb the water. Where possible, in a vegetable garden for example, where plants are grown in lines or blocks, a small trench running along the side of the row will act like a canal or irrigation ditch.

When you plant a tree or choice shrub, cut a small length (60 cm) of perforated drainage pipe and place it in the hole to the side of the root system. The top of the pipe should be just above soil level. You can then apply water down this pipe so that it goes directly to the roots.

Water butts are a simple and inexpensive way of collecting rainwater. Don't be afraid of using washing up or bath water except on acid loving plants (the water is alkaline) or on clay soils (the soaps in the water can cement the clay particles together).

If watering everything during dry weather is impossible, concentrate your efforts into nurturing those plants at most risk. These would include any new plantings and established plants with shallow roots or large leaves. Water these first and perhaps prune back to reduce leaf area.

Special consideration should be given to your choice plants (such as rhododendrons or Japanese maples) that would be expensive to replace.

If your lawn goes completely brown do not panic – it is not dead and will quickly green up with the first rains.

In the fruit garden try at least to water when fruit is developing. This is a crucial time when the plants need more water to swell the fruit.

Lots of containers can be a nightmare in a drought. In such circumstances, move them all together, close to the house or outside tap to make watering a little quicker. Have a gap between the top of the pot and the surface of the compost. This gives you a reservoir in which to hold water. Porous-sided containers such as terracotta dry out more quickly than plastic. Keep this in mind when you have to ration out water. The best way to re-moisten smaller and lighter pots that you are able to lift is to dunk them in a water butt or sink. This forces water back into the compost under pressure.

There are various automatic watering systems available these days. They comprise seep hoses or trickle or spray nozzles and battery-powered timers that stop and start the water supply exactly when required. They can be used in a greenhouse or in outdoor borders. They conserve water because if used properly, they can supply adequate water in accurate amounts.

8. Plant selection

If you know a little about where a plant grows wild, it will help you determine whether it will suit the conditions that prevail in your own plot. The most successful garden plantings are those that mimic a plant's natural habitat. If you want an easy life, don't try to grow rhododendrons in a chalky soil. Likewise don't plant moisture-loving plants in a dry garden.

RUE ENJOYS DRY CONDITIONS.

Many regions of the world are naturally dry and plants native to these areas have evolved to cope with arid conditions. Plants which tolerate dry conditions are called xerophytes. They have developed a number of characteristics which enable them to cope with a lack of water. Some xerophytes have a deep or tap root system which searches out water at greater depths in the soil (e.g. Eucalyptus).

Other plants have leaf adaptations to reduce water loss. Silver-leaved plants are actually covered in masses of tiny hairs or a sort of 'wool''. These trap moisture and increase humidity above the leaf surface and so reduce the need for the plant to transpire (e.g. Artemisia).

Smooth, waxy leaves, usually glaucous or blue in colour, perform a similar function (e.g. Rue and *Crambe maritima*).

Grasses and pine trees have rolled leaves which are greatly reduced in surface area. These have also evolved to reduce water stress.

There may not be leaves at all. Over the years, some plants have developed to such an extent that they have permanently shed their leaves, developing them in some cases into spines or prickles. Other groups of plants have reduced their leaves to just scales on flattened stems called cladodes (e.g. *Ruscus*).

An obvious adaptation to tolerate dryness can be seen in succulent plants. These store water in the leaves and stems just like a camel. Cacti are the most obvious example, but it is surprising how many hardy plants (for instance saxifrage and *Sedum*) have the same fat parts.

Plants with underground storage organs are also able to tolerate dry conditions. These are species with some sort of swollen stem or root system such as a bulb, corm, tuber or rhizome.

Many bulbous plants have evolved to tolerate the Mediterranean type of climate which crops up all over the world – South Africa, California, Southern and Western Australia and southern Chile as well as the 'Med' itself – and which is characterized by short wettish springs followed by long, hot, dry summers. Dahlias, potatoes, and daffodils, with their subterranean stores of food, are able to 'hide' underground during the hot, dry weather, conserving energy but maintaining the power to shoot up into flower as soon as the first drops of rain fall.

The Directory and Checklists that follow are full of plants with such adaptations. Many plants that like dry conditions positively hate the wet. A few tolerate both which means they are ideal for heavy clay soils (see Checklists)

Using drought-tolerant ground cover plants is a good idea too. These sprawling or spreading plants help suppress weed competition and keep the soil surface shaded and cool thereby reducing evaporation.

PREVIOUS PAGES: A HOT, DRY BORDER OF PERENNIALS.

PLANTS DIRECTORY

Pasiflora caerulea

A selection of some of the best plants
that tolerate dry conditions.
Most of the plants listed will also grow
where moisture is present.

Plants are listed in alphabetical order of Latin name
followed by the common name, if any. The common name is
excluded if it is identical to the Latin name.

The 'fact line' shows, in order:
Size – average height in metres and spread in metres of a
mature plant
Soil – tolerances, preferences or special requirements
Site – tolerances, preferences or special requirements

Acanthus spinosus

ACANTHUS BEAR'S BREECHES
Handsome perennials with large, glossy green leaves, deeply divided in some species. The tall pink or mauve flower spikes are spiny and appear in late summer. *A. mollis* and *A. spinosus* are the two normally seen. Both need plenty of room as they are apt to spread.

1.0 to 1.4 × 0.6 to 0.9   Dry, sandy soil   Sun

ALLIUM ORNAMENTAL ONION
A delightful genus of bulbs usually with 'balls' of flowers on top of slender stalks. The better species include:

A. aflatunense – lilac flowers in late May.

A. christophii (syn. *A. albopilosum*) – fantastic metallic violet-pink globes of flowers on short stalks in summer.

A. giganteum – lilac-purple flowers on, as the Latin name suggests, very tall stems.

The leaves of onions are a problem. After or even during flowering they start to brown and wither at the ends. Plant so that they are masked by other foliage.

0.3 to 1.2 × 0.15 to 0.30   Well-drained, fertile soil   Sun

ALYSSUM

Both the annual (*A. maritimum*, now correctly *Lobularia maritima*) and the perennial (*A. saxatile*, syn. *Aurinia saxatilis*) alyssum tolerate dry conditions and are often seen growing amongst paving slabs or in rock gardens. There are white, pink and purple flowered forms of the annual species which seed themselves around. The perennial has yellow flowers (in summer) and greyish leaves.

0.2 × 0.4   Poor, well-drained soil   Open, sunny site

ANTHEMIS PUNCTATA subsp. CUPANIANA

A vigorous ground-smothering perennial with silver (orange-scented) filigree foliage and masses of joyful white daisies from April through to June. A small plant is capable of covering over a square metre in the first growing season. Very good value.

0.3 × 0.9   Well-drained soil   Full sun

Allium giganteum

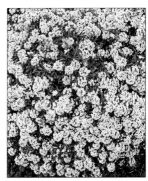

Alyssum maritimum

ARGYRANTHEMUM PARIS DAISY OR MARGUERITE

An ugly name but a beautiful plant. Formerly listed under chrysanthemum, from May to August these tender, woody perennials give an endless display of daisies above divided, sometimes silvery leaves. Ideal for containers. Protect in winter or take cuttings in September. *A. frutescens* is the common species but now many forms are readily available, in particular:

A. 'Vancouver' – pink turning to blush, double.

A. 'Rollason's Red' – single, rose-red.

A. 'Jamaica Primrose' – single, pale-yellow.

0.9 × 0.9   Well-drained   Sun

ARTEMISIA SOUTHERNWOOD OR WORMWOOD, ETC

A very important group of aromatic, silver or grey-leafed perennials that thrive in a dry position. Leaf shapes vary from feathery and filigree to willow-like.

A. absinthium 'Lambrook Silver' – the best form of Wormwood with greyish leaves.

A. ludoviciana var. *latiloba* – superb, almost white leaves that are long and narrow with jagged sides.

A. 'Powis Castle' – a larger, woody hybrid forming a dome of silver, deeply cut leaves.

All are excellent for 'cooling down' a hot-coloured border.

0.5 to 0.9 × 0.6   Well-drained   Sun

ASPHODELINE LUTEA ASPHODEL

An unusual perennial that can be quite a talking point. Early in the season the narrow, blue-grey foliage looks like an ornamental grass. Then, in late spring, a small fist-like flower spike shoots up and opens to reveal golden-yellow star-like flowers of great beauty.

0.9 × 0.3   Well-drained   Sun

BERBERIS BARBERRY

Tough and thorny evergreen or deciduous shrubs that will

Anthemis punctata subsp. *cupaniana*

Argyranthemum 'Vancouver'

Argyranthemum 'Jamaica Primrose'

Artemisia ludoviciana

Asphodeline lutea

Bergenia cordifolia 'Purpurea'

Buddleja davidii var. *nanhoensis* 'Nanho Blue'

grow anywhere. There are purple- and grey-leaved species. Many of the deciduous types have good autumn foliage tints. The normally yellow or orange flowers are followed, on many forms, by attractive red, pink, blue or black fruits. *B. thunbergii* and its many named varieties is perhaps the most popular, closely followed by *B. darwinii* and *B.* × *stenophylla*, both of which are evergreens that make fine hedges.

0.5 to 4.0 × 0.5 to 3.0   Any well-drained soil   Sun or part shade

BERGENIA ELEPHANT'S EARS OR MEGASEA
A useful evergreen perennial for covering the ground in awkward locations, such as bone-dry banks or dusty shade under trees. The large, rounded leaves that may turn to red or yellow in colder weather are the nearest textural substitute to hostas where they would shrivel and die. The bright pink, red or white flowers appear in late winter or spring.
B. cordifolia – the most common species; 'Purpurea' is a good variety.

B. 'Silberlicht' – the best white-flowered variety
B. 'Ballawley' – very large leaves and crimson blooms.

0.2 to 0.4 × 0.3 to 0.6   Any soil except boggy   Sun or shade

BUDDLEJA BUTTERFLY OR BOMBSITE BUSH

Tough, grow-anywhere deciduous shrubs with sweetly-scented flowers much loved by butterflies and other insects. The vigorous growth creates a rapid screen but regular pruning is needed for good flowering. *B. davidii* is the species normally seen in all its many coloured forms. Other species should be sought, including those that are slightly tender if you can provide them with a sunny wall, including *B. crispa* which has lavender-purple flowers and felted leaves and stems.

3.0 × 2.5   Any well-drained soil   Any site

CALAMINTHA NEPETA subsp. NEPETA (syn. C. NEPETOIDES)

The small lilac-white flowers last all summer on this tenacious little perennial and are borne in great profusion. Ideal for the front of a hot, dry border and more readily available than 20 or 30 years ago.

0.4 × 0.3   Well-drained   Sun

Calamintha nepeta subsp. *nepeta*

Campsis grandiflora

CAMPSIS TRUMPET VINE OR CREEPER

An ideal climber for a warm, dry wall. The hot, bright, orange-red trumpet-shaped flowers are produced in late summer, especially in poor soil. *C. grandiflora* is more often seen than *C. radicans* but the hybrid between these two (*C. × tagliabuana*) is excellent, especially the variety 'Mme Galen'.

2.0 × 2.0   Well-drained, poor   Warm sun

CEANOTHUS CALIFORNIAN LILAC

Evergreen and deciduous flowering wall shrubs preferring a sheltered, frost-free position and mainly providing those shades of blue all too rare in a garden. They actually thrive in poor, stony soils except where chalk is near the surface. They are often described as wall-shrubs, meaning that they appreciate the protection and support of a south-facing wall. Some varieties however have a low arching habit (e.g. *C. thyrisiflorus* var. *repens*) which can be used to grow over the edge of a raised bed or low wall. In full flower, which can occur, depending on the species, in spring, summer or autumn, the effect can be staggering with so many flowers that the leaves are obscured. There are many to choose from, *C. impressus,*

C. 'Italian Skies' and C. 'Gloire de Versailles' being the best of those that are easily obtained.

> 2.0 to 4.0 × 2.0 to 3.0   Well-drained, not shallow chalk
> Warm sun

....

CISTUS ROCK ROSE

Small evergreen shrubs that like nothing better than a parched bank or baked border. Most have greyish aromatic foliage and simple white, purple or pink flowers with a central boss of

Ceanothus thyrisflorus var. *repens*

yellow stamens that appear for less than a day, all through summer. *C.* × *purpureus* is one of the hardiest and *C.* 'Silver Pink' one of the prettiest.

1.0 × 1.0   Free-draining soils including chalk   Full sun

CROCUS

The many forms of *C. vernus*, spring flowering and highly bred, are most commonly seen, but other species, more delicate in form and colour, provide a welcome carpet of blooms from August through to February. *C. speciosus* is the best autumn flowering species, and in winter *C. chrysanthus* comes to the fore. Excellent in containers or in dappled shade under trees.

0.15 × 0.10   Well-drained soil   Sun or light shade

CYTISUS BROOM

Prostrate or medium-sized shrubs with (except for one species) tiny leaves and green stems. The brightly coloured pea flowers appear mainly in late spring or early summer. There is a wide range of named hybrids. All are best pruned after flowering but not into old wood.

0.5 to 2.5 × 0.5 to 2.0   Poor, well-drained avoiding extreme acid or alkaline   Sun

DICTAMNUS ALBUS DITTANY OR BURNING BUSH

This is a choice perennial that is seldom seen but worth tracking down. The aromatic leaves give off a volatile gas on warm days but it is the wonderful flowers, produced in early summer, that are the main attraction. They are white, produced on tall, erect spikes. *D.a.* var. *purpureus* has pale mauve flowers. Slow to establish but very long-lived.

0.9 × 0.6   Well-drained but fertile and not too acidic Sun or light shade

DOROTHEANTHUS MESEMBRYANTHEMUM OR LIVINGSTONE DAISY

This half-hardy annual will grow in almost pure sand. The

Cistus × purpureus

Crocus tommasinianus

Dictamnus albus var. *purpureus*

Dorotheanthus bellidiflorus

Eleagnus pungens 'Maculata'

brightly coloured daisies open when the sun is shining from July to September. It is normally sold in a colour mixture that will include white, pink, red, orange and yellow, so plant out in a bold mass, preferably isolated from other plants which will almost certainly clash with it. Ideal for parched banks or gravel beds.

0.1 × 0.2   Sandy soil   Full sun

DORYCNIUM HIRSUTUM
A delightful evergreen or semi-evergreen shrublet covered in fine, silky hairs (*hirsutum* means hairy) which give the whole plant a greyish hue. The small pea flowers are pink in bud, opening to white in summer. Readily available but under-rated.

0.4 × 0.5   Light soil   Sun

ELAEAGNUS OLEASTER
Tough evergreen or deciduous shrubs, resistant to high winds including those that are laden with salt in coastal districts. *E.*

Eryngium alpinum

pungens and *E. × ebbingei* and their forms are the most popular species. All are evergreen and medium sized; many are variegated. A little further investigation will reveal a few other species worth trying. *E. macrophylla* has large, rounded leaves that are metallic silver in colour. Most *Elaeagnus* have small flowers that would be easily missed but for their sweet fragrance.

1.5 to 4.0 × 1.5 to 2.5   Light soil but not shallow chalk
Sun or part shade

ERYNGIUM SEA HOLLY

Unmistakable perennials with prickly, thistle-like flower heads that can be dried. *E. maritmum* is a British native of coastal sand dunes with blue flowers and blue-grey spiny leaves. *E. alpinum* is perhaps the most beautiful species in flower, large, blue and very frilly. Leaf shape, colour and overall size varies greatly within the genus but all are suitable for dry sunny borders and poor sandy soils.

0.6 to 1.2 × 0.3 to 0.6   Any well-drained soil   Sun

EUPHORBIA SPURGE

A large and important group of perennials that attract much attention but demand little. All have a milky sap that can cause a rash so be careful when pruning or cutting for the house. Size and shape varies greatly from large, almost shrub-like domes to compact hummocks or ground sprawlers. Examples include:

E. amygdaloïdes var. *robbiae* – an evergreen clump-forming species with green flowers that thrives in dry shade.

E. characias – a magnificent grey-leaved woody evergreen with large spikes of green flowers with brown centres.

E. myrsinites – a spreader with blue-grey leaves. Ideal for sunny banks and dry walls, it looks like a miniature and prostrate *Eucalyptus*.

0.3 to 1.2 × 0.3 to 1.0   Well-drained but fertile   Sun or part shade

FESTUCA GLAUCA BLUE FESCUE

This is one of many ornamental grasses that tolerate dry conditions but which are yet to be fully utilized in our gardens. A few species of grasses that are invasive thugs have given the whole group a bad reputation, yet most are hummock-forming, highly attractive and no bother at all. This fescue has very fine, steel-blue leaves and is ideal for the front of a dry border.

0.4 × 0.3   Any well-drained soil   Sun

GALTONIA CANDICANS SUMMER HYACINTH

A summer-flowering bulb with greyish leaves. The blooms are white, hanging and bell-like on an erect spike.

1.2 × 0.3   Well-drained but fertile soil   Sun

GENISTA BROOM

These are mainly deciduous shrubs with the same common name as the closely related *Cytisus*. All have yellow, pea-shaped flowers in common, but little else.

G. aetnensis – the Mount Etna Broom is virtually a tree with dark green twigs. The flowers are fragrant.

Euphorbia characias subsp. *wulfenii*

Euphorbia myrsinites

Genista hispanica

Galtonia candicans

Hebe 'Midsummer Beauty'

Helianthemum

G. hispanica – Spanish Gorse is a prickly green mound that tolerates extreme drought.
G. tinctoria – the native Dyer's Greenweed is a small shrub with a popular double-flowered variety.

0.3 to 4.0 × 0.4 to 3.0   Poor, well-drained especially neutral to acid   Sun

HEBE SHRUBBY VERONICA
Evergreen, slightly tender shrubs from New Zealand, Australia and South America. They are spring to autumn flowering (mainly white) and tolerate exposed, windy sites and poor soils. Cold winter damage can occur but they usually sprout from lower down.
H. albicans – a splendid dwarf with grey-blue leaves.
H. hulkeana – perhaps the prettiest species with purple-blue, airy flower panicles. It is at its toughest when grown in a poor, well-drained soil.
H. salicifolia – a medium-sized bush with willow-like leaves. Very free flowering.

0.5 to 3.00 × 0.5 to 2.0   Well-drained   Warm sun or light shade

HELIANTHEMUM SUN ROSE
Dwarf, mainly evergreen or ever-grey shrubs that make excellent ground-cover. The brightly coloured flowers are like

miniature versions of those found on the related genus of *Cistus*. They are ideal for rock gardens or the dry border's edge. Varieties include:

'Henfield Brilliant' – bright orange flowers and grey-green foliage.

'The Bride' – cream and yellow with silver foliage.

'Wisley Primrose' – lemon flowers and greyish foliage.

0.3 × 1.5   Well-drained   Sun

HELICHRYSUM PETIOLARE

This is a tender, woody perennial now popular as a summer bedding plant, especially for tubs and hanging baskets, where its small, rounded, grey-haired leaves provide a perfect foil to any colour scheme. There is a yellow-leaved ('Limelight') and a variegated form. *H. italicum* subsp. *serotinum* is the hardy curry plant, with sage-green leaves smelling of Indian food.

0.3 × 1.0   Well-drained   Sun or part shade

HYPERICUM

A large group of summer and autumn flowering shrubs or ground-cover plants. All have bright yellow flowers and fresh green leaves. *H. calycinum* is the ubiquitous Rose of Sharon

Hypericum calycinum

Ipomoea

that can be an invasive pest in a small garden. Given room, it is a fine ground-cover that will even tolerate being cut back by a hover-mower. Sadly, a serious rust has affected it in recent years. *H.* 'Hidcote' is an excellent flowering shrub with a neat rounded habit.

0.3 to 1.5 × 0.5 to 2.0   Well-drained but fertile   Sun or shade

IPOMOEA MORNING GLORY
This is the famous half-hardy annual climber with heart-shaped leaves and large blue and white bindweed-like flowers. It is a rapid grower from seed, ideal for trellis panels or small pergolas.

1.0 × 2.0   Well-drained   Sheltered and full sun

LAVANDULA LAVENDER
One of the most popular evergreen or semi-evergreen sub-shrubs of all time. It has grey-green aromatic foliage with mainly blue flowers appearing throughout summer. *L. angusti-folia* and *L.* × *intermedia* are the commonest and have long been cultivated. *L. stoechas*, French lavender, which is slightly tender, has attractive purple flowers with strange, protruding bracts. They are especially pronounced on the subspecies *pedunculata*. All are excellent in containers, as low hedges or as

full stop or corner plants in a border. There are many varieties of garden hybrids. Those with pink or white flowers are less satisfactory, while the notable blues include:

L. angustifolia 'Hidcote' – compact, violet-blue flowers in early July.

L. 'Munstead' – compact, lavender-blue flowers in late June.

L. × *intermedia* Dutch Group – Dutch lavender, large with light lavender flowers, late July.

0.3 to 0.6 × 0.4   Any soil except heavy clay or boggy conditions
Sun or a little shade

LIBERTIA FORMOSA

A superb evergreen perennial with grass-like leaves and white saucer shaped flowers in early summer. Its stalwart stature and permanent foliage belies its preference for milder districts.

0.9 × 0.6   Well-drained   Sun or part shade

Lavandula angustifolia 'Hidcote'

LIMONIUM PLATYPHYLLUM STATICE OR SEA LAVENDER
This is the true perennial statice with thin stems holding masses of tiny lavender-coloured flowers above leathery leaves in late summer. As with the annual statice, the flowers dry well. It is a coastal plant native to the Black Sea region and tolerates poor soils and periods of drought.

0.4 × 0.5   Well-drained soils including chalk   Sun

LINUM NARBONENSE PERENNIAL FLAX
A small-leaved perennial with erect stems that produce the most beautiful azure-blue flowers from May to July. It will live longer in sandy soil, especially if in a sheltered spot.

0.4 × 0.6 Well-drained Sheltered, sun

LIRIOPE MUSCARI
An evergreen perennial that is often mistaken for a grass, due to its tufted habit and arching, linear leaves. Consequently, the dense spikes of bright violet flowers in autumn can be a surprising sight. It is a versatile plant especially suited to dry shade.

0.3 × 0.4   Any reasonably drained soil   Sun or shade

LYCHNIS CORONARIA ROSE CAMPION OR
DUSTY MILLER
A fine perennial covered in grey wool with red-purple flowers in summer. It rarely needs staking and will even grow in gravelly soils and spread itself around by seed. There is a white variety ('Alba') and a white with a cerise centre ('Oculata').

0.9 × 0.5   Well-drained, fertile   Sun

NERINE BOWDENII
Planted at the base of a warm wall, this South African bulb is perfectly hardy. The bright pink lily-like flowers appear in autumn when the flower garden is at a low ebb. There are a few selected forms for the connoisseur, including a good white.

0.6 × 0.3   Dry soils   Warm, full sun

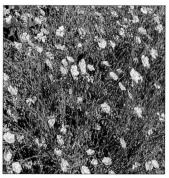

Linum narbonense

Liriope muscari

Nerine bowdenii

Osteospermum 'Pink Whirls'

OSTEOSPERMUM

A tender sub-shrub usually grown as a summer bedding plant. At least one species (*O. jucundum*) will survive a mild winter without protection, especially in coastal regions. All flower for a considerable time (May to September) and there are many good forms available. *O. jucundum* has mauve flowers, others are white, pink, white with blue centres and soft yellow. A few have extraordinary spoon-shaped or quilled petals (e.g. 'Whirligig' and 'Pink Whirls'). 'Silver Sparkler' has variegated leaves. All make excellent pot plants, border 'fillers' or conservatory plants. A new variety, 'Stardust', bred in Yorkshire, is said to be completely hardy.

0.4 × 0.4   Well-drained   Warm, sun

....

PASSIFLORA PASSION FLOWER

A large genus of woody climbers with a few able to grow outside in Britain in warm locations. *P. caerulea* is one of the hardiest species with blue flowers along with a variety, 'Constance Elliott', that has white flowers. The complex flower structure defies description. The common name derives

Phormium

from their resemblance to the various instruments of Christ's Passion. The nails, wounds, crown of thorns and even the ten of the twelve apostles (excluding Peter and Judas) are supposedly represented. On a warm wall, growth is rapid and flowering profuse. It also makes an excellent conservatory plant.

3.0 × 2.0   Dry, fertile soil   Warm, sheltered

PHLOMIS FRUTICOSA JERUSALEM SAGE
A small shrub covered in grey-green wool. The bright yellow flowers appear in whorls up stiff branches in early summer. Ideal for dry sunny banks with other grey foliage and perhaps blue flowers. 'Edward Bowles' is an improved hybrid with larger leaves and softer flowers.

1.2 × 1.2   Well-drained   Sun

PHORMIUM NEW ZEALAND FLAX
Striking plants with large, sword-like leaves that give a lush 'tropical' effect. They hate cold and wet winters when the roots can rot away. Dry, sandy soils and a mulch to insulate from winter freezing are the ideal combination. The strange

red flowers are produced on tall black stems. *P. tenax* is larger than *P. cookianum*, and there are a number of named varieties and hybrids with purple or variously striped leaves.

1.0 to 2.0 × 0.3 to 0.9   Dry soil   Warm sun

ROSA RUGOSA JAPANESE ROSE

The parent of a distinct class of roses with large open flowers that are richly scented and long-lasting. The leaves are luxuriant and deeply veined. Most have a suckering habit. They are tough and disease-free, tolerating harsh, windy sites and poor soils. Autumn tints are good and the hips are the size, shape and colour of small tomatoes. 'Fru Dagmar Hastrup' has clear pink flowers and is perhaps the toughest of all. 'Max Graf' is a fine ground-cover rose with pink flowers fading to white.

1.0 to 3.0 × 1.5 to 2.0   Any soil   Sun or part shade

SANTOLINA LAVENDER COTTON

Compact dwarf shrubs with feathery foliage that is aromatic and yellow or cream flowers in summer. *S. chamaecyparissus* is the usual species, with bright yellow flowers. *S. pinnata* has varieties with softer flowers, 'Edward Bowles' and 'Sulphurea'. The lavender cottons positively hate moisture and manure.

0.8 × 0.8   Poor, sandy soils   Sun

SEDUM STONECROP

Succulent-leaved perennials with a compact upright or prostrate habit. A number are best described as small alpine or rock garden plants (such as *S. acre*) that prefer dry conditions, as do the larger, border varieties including *S.* 'Autumn Joy' (pink flowers in early autumn) and the various forms of *S. spectabile*.

0.3 to 0.6 × 0.3 to 0.6   Any soil   Sun

SEMPERVIVUM HOUSELEEK

An evergreen miniature for rock gardens, dry stone walls or tiled roofs. Rosettes of succulent leaves form in clusters and

Rosa rugosa 'Roseraie de l'Haÿ'

Sempervivum tectorum

Senecio 'Sunshine'

Sedum 'Autumn Joy'

Solanum crispum 'Glasnevin'

throw up leafy stems that terminate in large star-like flowers in June and July. *S. tectorum* is the best known species. Some varieties have leaves tinted bronze or ruby.

0.10 × 0.20   Very well-drained soil   Sun

SENECIO 'SUNSHINE'

This is the most common member of a large group of ever-green mainly downy-leaved shrubs with yellow (or occasionally white) daisy flowers. 'Sunshine' is often listed as *S. greyi*, but is more correctly classed as a member of a group known as the Dunedin Hybrids. Just to confuse the issue further, botanists are now telling us that many senecios, including 'Sunshine', should be called *Brachyglottis*. Whatever the name,

Spartium junceum

this is an excellent plant for any dry garden, especially those that are exposed to high winds, including those that are salty.

1.0 × 2.0   Well-drained   Exposed, sun

SOLANUM CRISPUM

A semi-evergreen climber related to the potato with its rich purple-blue flowers with a beak-like centre of yellow stamens from July to September. Its vigour enables it to cover large areas of wall, fence or shed very quickly. The variety 'Glasnevin' flowers for even longer.

4.0 × 3.0   Any soil except chalk   Warm wall

SPARTIUM JUNCEUM   SPANISH BROOM

Another shrubby member of the pea family, closely related to *Genista* and *Cytisus*. It is strong growing with small inconspicuous leaves, green, rush-like stems and large, fragrant yellow pea-flowers that appear throughout summer. It is an excellent coastal plant.

3.0 × 2.0   Well-drained   Sun

STACHYS BYZANTINA   LAMB'S EARS

This is a spreading perennial with silver-grey foliage and stems. The flowers are small, magenta-pink in colour and produced on woolly spikes. It is an excellent ground cover or front of border plant.

0.5 × 0.3   Well-drained   Sun

STIPA

This is an important group of ornamental grasses that withstand cold and exposed positions as long as the soil is reasonably fertile. *S. arundinacea* forms an evergreen clump of arching leaves that is wider than it is high. For much of the year the foliage is tinted bronze and gold. *S. gigantea* is a giant grass with grey-green leaves and oat-like flower spikes.

0.4 to 1.8 × 0.4 to 1.2   Well-drained, fertile   Sun

TAMARIX TAMARISK
The tamarisks are tough, wind-resisting shrubs with slender branches and small plumes of foliage. The tiny pink flowers appear in summer. They respond well to hard pruning; left alone they make sparsely branched trees that provide less shelter. *T. ramosissima* is widely available as the varieties 'Rosea' or 'Rubra' which have darker coloured flowers.

3.0 × 3.0   Well-drained   Sun

TEUCRIUM GERMANDER
A small but variable group of shrubs most commonly represented in gardens by *T. × lucidrys*, the wall germander, which has dark green aromatic leaves and small pink flowers, and *T. fruticans*, the shrubby germander, which has an open lax habit, greyish leaves and stems and pale blue flowers. The latter needs some protection in harsh winters.

0.4 to 1.0 × 0.4 to 1.0   Well-drained   Sun

THYMUS THYME
Evergreen herbs with either a creeping or upright habit and tiny, aromatic leaves and purple flowers. Ideal for containers, raised beds or left to spread amongst slabs or brickwork.

0.2 × 0.2   Well-drained, especially chalk   Sun

YUCCA
Spiky leaved evergreen shrubs with a strong architectural form that provides a welcome contrast to the average perennial or shrub habit. The cream or white flowers are produced on rigid spikes in summer or autumn. *Y. filamentosa* is hardy and versatile with greyish leaves and fragrant flowers. *Y. gloriosa* has stiff, pointed leaves that will stab, so do not plant it next to a path. There is a fine variegated variety.

1.5 × 1.0   Well-drained   Sun

Stipa gigantea

Tamarix tetandra

Thymus richardii subsp. *nitidus* 'Peter Davis'

Stachys byzantina

Yucca gloriosa 'Variegata'

PLANT CHECKLISTS

··

A FINGERTIP GUIDE TO PLANTS
FOR A DRY GARDEN

PLANTS FOR DRY SHADE

Acanthus Bear's Breeches
Ajuga Bugle
Alchemilla mollis Lady's Mantle
Anemone nemorosa Wood
  Anemone
Anemone × hybrida Japanese
  Anemone
Arrhenatherum elatius Ornamental
  Grass
Aucuba spp.
Berberis Barberry
Bergenia Elephant's Ears
Brunnera macrophylla Perennial
  Forget-me-not
Chaenomeles Flowering Quince
Chionodoxa Glory of the Snow
Choisya ternata Mexican Orange
  Blossom
Colchicum speciosum Meadow
  Saffron
Convallaria majalis Lily-of-the-
  Valley
Cornus alba Dogwood
Cotoneaster
Crocus
Cyclamen
Danaë racemosa Alexandrian Laurel
Dicentra Bleeding Heart
Doronicum Leopard's Bane

Epimedium
Eranthis hyemalis Winter Aconite
Euonymus fortunei Spindle Bush
Euphorbia amygdaloïdes var. *robbiae*
  Mrs Robb's Bonet
Fatsia japonica
Galanthus nivalis Snowdrop
Gaultheria shallon
Geranium Crane's-bill
Hebe Shrubby Veronica
Hedera Ivy
Helictotrichon sempervirens
  Ornamental Grass
Hyacinthoides non-scripta Bluebell
Hypericum calycinum Rose of
  Sharon
Iris foetidissima Stinking Iris
Lamium Dead Nettle or
  Archangel
Leucojum Snowflake
Ligustrum ovalifolium Large-leaved
  Garden Privet
Lonicera pileata Honeysuckle
Lunaria annua Honesty
Mahonia aquifolum Oregon Grape
Miscanthus Ornamental Grass
Muscari Grape Hyacinth
Narcissus Daffodil
Omphalodes cappadocica
Osmanthus delavayi
Pachysandra terminalis

Persicaria affine Knotweed
Photinia davidiana
Polygonatum multiflorum Solomon's Seal
Prunus laurocerasus 'Otto Luyken'
Pulmonaria Lungwort
Pyracantha Firethorn
Ruscus aculeatus Butcher's Broom
Sambucus nigra and *S. racemosa* varieties Elder
Sarcococca Christmas Box
Saxifraga × *urbium* London Pride
Scilla Squill
Skimmia
Symphoricarpos Snowberry
Symphytum grandiflorum Comfrey
Tellima grandiflora
Tiarella cordifolia
Viburnum opulus Guelder Rose
Viburnum tinus Laurustinus
Vinca Periwinkle
Waldsteinia ternata

Eryngium giganteum and
Eryngium tripartitum.

PLANTS FOR VERY HOT BORDERS

Achillea Yarrow
Alyssum
Artemisia Southernwood, Wormwood, etc
Aubrieta
Berberis Barberry
Buddleja Butterfly Bush
Calamintha nepeta subsp. *nepeta*
Campsis Trumpet Vine
Ceanothus Californian Lilac
Cistus Rock Rose
× *Cupressocyparis leylandii* Leyland Cypress
Cytisus Broom
Eryngium Sea Holly
Euphorbia Spurge
Foeniculum vulgare Fennel
Genista Broom
Gypsophila Baby's Breath
Helianthemum Sun Rose
Iris pallida
Juniperus Juniper
Lavandula Lavender
Linum narbonense Flax
Malva Mallow
Nepeta Catmint
Osteospermum
Passiflora Passion Flower
Philadelphus Mock Orange
Robinia pseudoacacia False Acacia
Rosmarinus officinalis Rosemary
Salvia officinalis Sage
Sedum Stonecrop
Sempervivum Houseleek
Solanum crispum
Spartium junceum Spanish Broom
Stachys byzantina Lamb's Ears
Stipa
Tanacetum haradjanii
Taxus baccata Common Yew
Thymus Thyme
Yucca

PLANTS FOR HEAVY CLAY SOIL (WET IN WINTER, DRY IN SUMMER)

Acer platanoides Norway Maple
Aesculus parviflora Horse Chestnut
Alchemilla mollis Lady's Mantle
Alnus Alder
Amelanchier Snowy Mespilus
Arctostaphylos uva-ursi Red Barberry
Asphodeline lutea Asphodel
Bergenia Elephant's Ears
Betula Birch
Calamintha sepeta subsp. *nepeta*
Choisya ternata Mexican Orange Blossom
Cornus canadensis Creeping Dogwood
Corydalis lutea
Crataegus Hawthorn
Epimedium
Euphorbia griffithii Spurge
Filipendula hexapetala Dropwort
Geranium Crane's-bill
Iris foetidissima Stinking Iris
Leucanthemum maximum Shasta Daisy
Myrtus communis Myrtle
Osmanthus delavayi
Pachyphragma macrophyllum
Pachysandra terminalis
Philadelphus Mock Orange
Polygonatum multiflorum Solomon's Seal
Polygonum affine
Prunus laurocerasus Cherry Laurel
Prunus lusitanica Portugal Laurel
Pulmonaria Lungwort
Rubus tricolor Ornamental Bramble
Ruscus aculeatus Butcher's Broom
Sambucus Elder
Saponaria ocymoides Soapwort
Sorbus aucuparia Mountain Ash
Spiraea
Symphoricarpos Snowberry
Tellima grandiflora
Trachystemon orientale
Tradescantia
Valeriana phu 'Aurea'

TREES AND SHRUBS THAT WILL PROVIDE SHELTER FROM DRYING WINDS IN DRY SOILS

Acer pseudoplatanus Sycamore★
Berberis Barberry★
Betula Birch
Crataegus Hawthorn
× *Cupressocyparis leylandii* Leyland Cypress★
Cupressus macrocarpa Monterey Cypress★
Elaeagnus★
Eucalyptus★
Euonymus japonicus Japanese Spindle Bush★
Fuchsia magellenica Fuchsia★
Genista aetnensis Mount Etna Broom★
Griselinia littoralis★
Hebe (taller spp.) Shrubby Veronica★
Hippophaë rhamnoides Sea Buckthorn★
Ligustrum ovalifolium Large-leaved Privet★
Olearia Daisy Bush★
Osmanthus delavayi
Pinus nigra Austrian Pine★
Prunus lauroceracus Cherry Laurel
Prunus lusitanica Portugal Laurel

Rosa rugosa Japanese Rose★
Sambucus Elder
Sorbus aucuparia Mountain Ash
Spartium junceum Spanish Broom★
Tamarix Tamarisk★
Ulex europaeus Gorse

★Salt tolerant for coastal regions

ANNUALS AND BIENNIALS FOR DRY CONDITIONS

Many 'bedding' plants prefer dry conditions. The list below is a selection of the best.

Acroclinium Everlasting HHA
Amaranthus Love-lies-bleeding HHA
Antirrhinum Snapdragon HHA
Arctotis African Daisy HHA
Arctotis fastuosa Monarch of the Veldt HHA
Calandrinia umbellata HHA
Calendula Pot Marigold HA
Callistephus China Aster HHA
Cosmos Cosmea HHA

Echium Annual Borage HA
Erysimum Wallflower HB
Eschscholzia California Poppy HA
Gazania HHA
Ipomoea Morning Glory HHA
Limonium Statice HHA
Linaria maroccana Toadflax HA
Linum grandiflorum Flax HA
Lobularia maritima Sweet Alyssum HA
Malope trifida Malope HA
Mentzelia lindleyi (syn. *Bartonia aurea*) Blazing Star HA
Mesembryanthemum or *Dorotheanthus* Livingstone Daisy HHA
Phacelia HA
Portulaca grandiflora Sun Plant HHA
Tagetes Marigold HHA
Tropaeolum Nasturtium HA
Ursinia HHA
Verbascum Mullein HB

HA– Hardy Annual
HHA– Half-hardy Annual
HB– Biennial

Calendula

GROUND COVER PLANTS FOR DRY CONDITIONS

The plants listed below tolerate dryness and have a spreading habit which conserves moisture by reducing evaporation from the soil surface.

Alchemilla mollis Lady's Mantle
Alyssum saxatile Alyssum
Anthemis punctata subsp. *cupaniana*
Bergenia Elephants' Ears
Cerastium Snow in Summer
Cornus canadensis Creeping Dogwood
Cytisus (prostrate varieties) Broom
Epimedium
Euphorbia myrsinites Spurge
Euphorbia amygdaloïdes var. *robbiae* Mrs Robb's Bonnet
Hebe (some) Shrubby Veronica
Hedera helix Ivy
Helianthemum Sun Rose
Hypericum calycinum Rose of Sharon
Juniperus (prostrate varieties) Juniper
Lamium Dead Nettle or Archangel
Lonicera nitida Shrubby Honeysuckle
Pachysandra terminalis
Pulmonaria Lungwort
Rosa 'Max Graf' Japanese Rose (hybrid)
Rosa × *paulii* Japanese Rose (hybrid)
Stachys byzantina Lamb's Ears
Tellima grandiflora
Thymus Thyme

Tropaeolum Nasturtium
Vinca Periwinkle

TREES FOR DRY SOILS AND FOR WINDSWEPT SITES

Acer pseudoplatanus Sycamore
Cupressus macrocarpa Monterey Cypress
Eucalyptus
Genista aetnensis Mount Etna Broom
Pinus Pine
Populus alba White Poplar
Quercus ilex Holm Oak
Robinia False Acacia
Sorbus aria Whitebeam

PERENNIALS AND BULBS FOR DRY CONDITIONS

Acanthus Bear's Breeches
Achillea Yarrow
Agapanthus African Lily*†
Allium Ornamental Onion†
Alstroemeria Peruvian Lily*†
Alyssum saxatile Alyssum
Amaryllis belladonna Belladonna Lily†
Anthemis
Argyranthemum Paris Daisy or Marguerite*
Armeria Thrift
Artemisia Southernwood, Wormwood, etc
Asphodeline lutea Asphodel
Ballota pseudodictamnus *
Bergenia Elephant's Ears
Calamintha nepeta subsp. *nepeta*
Centranthus ruber Red Valerian

Cerastium Snow-in-Summer
Crocus
Dianthus Pink and Carnation
Dicentra Bleeding Heart
Dicttamus albus Dittany
Dryopteris filix-mas Male Fern
Eryngium Sea Holly
Erysimum Perennial Wallflower
Euphorbia Spurge
Festuca glauca Blue Fescue
Gaillardia
Galtonia candicans Summer
  Hyacinth
Gypsophila Baby's Breath
Helichrysum petiolare★
Iberis Candytuft
Iris unguicularis
Kniphofia Red Hot Poker
Lamium Dead Nettle or
  Archangel
Libertia formosa
Limonium latifolium Perennial
  Statice
Linum narbonense Flax
Liriope muscari
Lychnis coronaria Dusty Miller or
  Rose Campion
Malva Mallow
Nepeta Catmint

Nerine bowdenii†
Oenothera Evening Primrose
Origanum Marjoram
Osteospermum★
Pelargonium Geranium★
Phormium New Zealand Flax
Polypodium vulgare Polypody Fern
Ruta Rue
Salvia officinalis Sage
Sedum Stonecrop
Sempervivum Houseleek
Sisyrinchium striatum Satin Flower
Stachys byzantina Lamb's Ears
Stipa
Thymus Thyme
Tulipa Tulip†
Watsonia spp.★†
Yucca
Zauschneria Californian Fuchsia

★Perennials that are mainly used as
bedding plants due to being tender
or slightly tender. In milder areas
they may not need protection. In
colder areas they need to be
repropagated or lifted and
overwintered in a frost-free
environment.

†Bulbous perennials.

Argyranthemum

Philadelphus

SHRUBS FOR DRY SOILS AND/OR WINDSWEPT SITES

Atriplex halimus Sea Purslane
Berberis Barberry
Buddleja Butterfly Bush
Caryopteris
Ceanothus Californian Lilac
Cistus Rock Rose
Colutea arborescens Bladder Seuna
Coronilla glauca
Cytisus Broom
Dorycnium hirsutum
Elaeagnus
Euonymus Spindle Bush
Genista Broom
Halimium
Hebe Shrubby Veronica
Helianthemum Sun Rose
Helichrysum italicum subsp. *serotinum* Curry Plant
Hibiscus syriacus Syrian Ketmia
Hippophaë rhamnoides Sea Buckthorn
Hypericum
Lavandula Lavender

Lonicera nitida Shrubby Honeysuckle
Olearia Daisy Bush
Perovskia atriplicifolia Russian Sage
Philadelphus Mock Orange
Phlomis Jerusalem Sage and others
Phygelius capensis Cape Figwort
Potentilla
Prunus tenella Dwarf Russian Almond
Rhus Sumach
Ribes Flowering Currant
Rosa rugosa Japanese Rose
Rosmarinus officinalis Rosemary
Sambucus Elder
Santolina Lavender Cotton
Senecio
Spartium junceum Spanish Broom
Spiraea
Symphoricarpos Snowberry
Tamarix Tamarisk
Teucrium fruticans Shrubby Germander
Ulex europaeus Gorse

CLIMBERS FOR DRY SOILS

Bignonia capreolata Cross Vine★
Campsis Trumpet Vine★
Hedera Ivy
Ipomoea Morning Glory (annual)★
Jasminium Jasmine★
Mutisia★
Passiflora Passion Flower★
Polygonum baldschuanicum Russian Vine
Solanum spp.
Trachelospermum★
Vitis Grapevine

★Require the warmth of a south-facing wall

Beth Chatto Gardens

Useful Address

Horticultural Trades Association, 19 High Street, Theale, Reading, Berkshire RG7 5AH

(for details of suppliers of windbreaks, mulches, watering aids, etc)

Famous Dry Gardens to Visit

Beth Chatto Gardens, Elmstead Market, nr. Colchester, Essex
Denmans, Denmans Lane, Fontwell, West Sussex
Highdown Gardens, Worthing, East Sussex

PICTURE ACKNOWLEDGEMENTS

b–bottom/c–centre/l–left/r–right/t–top
Eric Crichton front cover background, Back cover, 5, 20,
23, 24-25, 29(r), 31(cl), 37(t & br), 41, 43, 47(tl), 51(tl & cr), 52,
55(t & cl), 59, 62
Jerry Harpur 1(Denmans), 63 (Beth Chatto)
Andrew Lawson 9, 11, 17, 28, 31(t & b), 34, 37(bl), 42, 44, 45, 48,
51(tr), 55(bl)
S. & O. Mathews 41(br), 47(tr), 55(br)
Clive Nichols front cover inset, 1, 27, 32(l), 35, 38, 39, 47(b), 49,
51(bl), 57
Photos Horticultural 14, 32(r)
Harry Smith Collection 29(l), 33, 51(br)
Peter Thurman 19